UNSOLVED MYSTERIES

Jack the Ripper

ABDO
Publishing Company

Jack the Ripper

THE PENNY
ILLUSTRATED PAPER
AND ILLUSTRATED TIMES

SKETCH OF THE MAN
WHO VISITED McLUSK

DOWES THE MITRE SQUARE VICTIM

By Jennifer Joline Anderson
Content Consultant
Dr. Drew Gray
Senior Lecturer, History of Crime
Northampton University

CREDITS

Published by ABDO Publishing Company, PO Box 398166, Minneapolis, MN 55439. Copyright © 2012 by Abdo Consulting Group, Inc. International copyrights reserved in all countries. No part of this book may be reproduced in any form without written permission from the publisher. The Essential Library™ is a trademark and logo of ABDO Publishing Company.

Printed in the United States of America,
North Mankato, Minnesota
102011
012012

 THIS BOOK CONTAINS AT LEAST 10% RECYCLED MATERIALS.

Editor: Melissa York
Copy Editor: Kathryn-Ann Geis
Series design: Becky Daum, Christa Schneider, & Ellen Schofield
Cover production: Christa Schneider
Interior production: Marie Tupy

Library of Congress Cataloging-in-Publication Data
Anderson, Jennifer Joline.
  Jack the Ripper / by Jennifer Joline Anderson.
    p. cm. -- (Unsolved mysteries)
  Includes bibliographical references and index.
  ISBN 978-1-61783-305-2
  1. Jack, the Ripper. 2. Serial murders--England-
-London--History--19th century. 3. Serial
murderers--England--London--History--19th century. 4.
Whitechapel (London, England)--History. I. Title.
  HV6535.G6L27 2012
  364.152'32092--dc23
                                2011038902

Table of Contents

Chapter 1   Murder in Whitechapel   6

Chapter 2   London's Mean Streets   16

Chapter 3   The Killer Strikes Again   24

Chapter 4   Double Event   34

Chapter 5   The Fifth and Final Murder?   48

Chapter 6   Ripper Fever   56

Chapter 7   Profile of a Killer   62

Chapter 8   The Suspects   70

Chapter 9   A Modern Look at the Crimes   84

  96

Tools and Clues   98

Timeline   102

Glossary   104

Additional Resources   106

Source Notes   110

Index   112

About the Author   112

About the Content Consultant

Chapter 1

Murder in Whitechapel

At the dark hour of 3:45 a.m. on August 31, 1888, a lone constable walked his beat along Buck's Row, a narrow cobblestone street in the East End of London. He had passed through this lane half an hour earlier, but this time, something was different. Ahead, in the dim light of the gas streetlamp, he saw what looked like a large bundle lying near a gateway at the side of the road. As he drew closer and shone his lantern on the object, he saw that the bundle was a woman—and that she had been savagely murdered. Her throat was slashed nearly from ear to ear, and blood was pooling beneath her lifeless body.

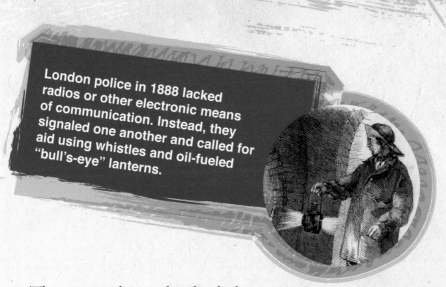

The woman lay on her back, her eyes open and her arms out to her sides. When the policeman touched her arm, he found it was still warm above the elbow, meaning she had been killed not long before he arrived.

Constable John Neil was soon joined by two other policeman who had been alerted by the flash of his lantern. They called for a doctor, who examined the

Searching for Clues

In 1888, police had few tools for crime investigation. Fingerprinting would not be used to solve crimes until some 14 years later. DNA analysis was not even dreamed of, so police were unable to analyze any physical evidence left by the killer, such as hair, skin, blood, or other bodily fluids. In 1888, they were not able to distinguish blood types or even tell human blood from animal blood, so if a suspect had been found with the victim's blood on his clothing, he could claim the blood was from an animal—there were many slaughterhouses in Whitechapel—and there would be no way to prove otherwise. The best hope police had of convicting a criminal was to locate an eyewitness or catch the killer in the act.

body and confirmed the victim had not been dead more than half an hour. But the killer had vanished without a trace. No fresh wheel marks could be seen on the road, nor any bloody footprints giving a clue as to where the killer had fled. There was no sign of struggle and no blood trail to indicate the body had been dragged or moved. It appeared she had been killed on the spot. And yet several people who lived in nearby apartments, when questioned, said they had heard no sound. Police concluded the victim had been caught by surprise and killed before she had a chance to scream.

Without a Sound, Without a Trace

One of the aspects of the Ripper's murders that baffled police was how swift and silent they were. Evidently, the killer caught his victims completely by surprise, and he may have strangled them first before cutting them.

The other mystery is how the killer was able to kill and mutilate his victims in public places without ever being spotted in the act. Initially, police theorized that he killed his victims in another location and dumped the bodies. However, evidence showed that all the victims were killed where they lay.

It was nearing dawn. The body was quickly wheeled away to a mortuary, where it could undergo a postmortem examination. As attendants removed the woman's clothing, they made another gruesome discovery. The cut to the woman's throat was not the only injury the killer had inflicted. There were stab wounds and a deep, jagged cut from rib cage to pelvis had ripped open her abdomen. The

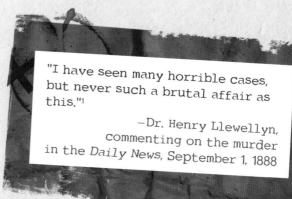

"I have seen many horrible cases, but never such a brutal affair as this."[1]

—Dr. Henry Llewellyn, commenting on the murder in the *Daily News*, September 1, 1888

attendants and doctor were horrified. What kind of monster had committed this crime?

A Date with Death

The next question was: Who was the victim? It was not an easy task to identify her, as the only belongings she carried were a pocket handkerchief, a comb, and a broken mirror. She was a small woman, approximately five feet two inches (1.6 m) tall, with dark brown hair turning to gray. Reports estimated her age to be in her early forties, though some accounts said she looked younger. Several of her teeth were missing. She wore multiple layers of clothing, indicating that she was probably homeless and wearing all the clothes she owned on her body. Stenciled on the waistband of her two petticoats were the words "Lambeth Workhouse." A workhouse was a place where the poor could do manual labor

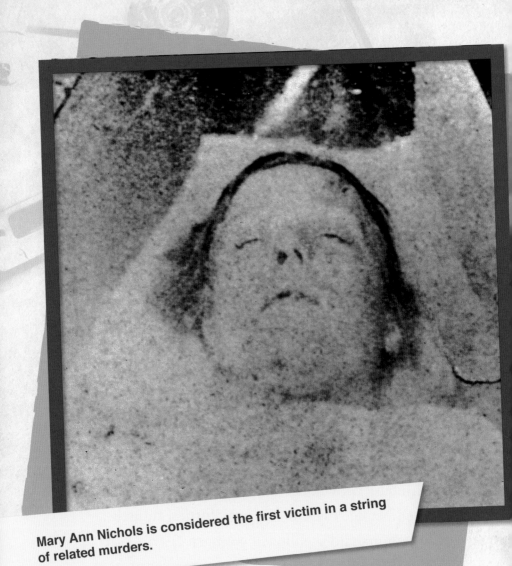

Mary Ann Nichols is considered the first victim in a string of related murders.

in exchange for food and a place to stay, so again, this was a clue that the woman was poor and had no permanent home.

Police began by asking around at local lodging houses and at the Lambeth Workhouse to see if anyone knew the victim. By the end of the day, women came forward who identified her as Mary Ann "Polly" Nichols. Nichols, age 42, had been married and had five children but was a heavy drinker. Her alcoholism had led to the breakup of her marriage, and she ended up on the streets, supporting herself through prostitution.

The police learned that Nichols had indeed been a resident of Lambeth Workhouse several months earlier. More recently, she had been staying at a doss, or lodging house for the poor, at 18 Thrawl Street. On the night of her murder, however, Nichols had spent all of her money drinking at the Frying Pan Pub and had nothing left with which to pay for a bed. She was not worried and boasted to the lodging-house keeper as she went back out to the street, "I'll soon get my doss money. See what a jolly bonnet I've got now!"[2] Nichols was wearing a new bonnet that made her feel especially pretty that night and felt she would easily attract a paying customer.

The last person to see her alive, apart from the killer, was Nichols's friend Ellen Holland, who ran into her at approximately 2:30 a.m. on a street corner. Holland tried to persuade Nichols to come

Nichols was found dead here in the gutter on Buck's Row.

back to the lodging house with her, but a drunken Nichols brushed her off, still confident she would find a date. Just over an hour later, Nichols was dead, her mutilated body left lying on the street less than one mile (1.6 km) away.

At the inquest into her death, those who knew Nichols said she had no enemies. She had not seen her husband for several years and was not attached to any particular man, so murder by a jealous spouse or boyfriend was not a plausible explanation. The killer's motive could not have been robbery, as Nichols was penniless. It was possible that Nichols had tried to steal from the murderer—she had a history of petty theft—but that would not explain the brutality of the attack against her. The motive, it appeared, was simply to kill and mutilate another human being. Nichols was in the wrong place at the wrong time. As a prostitute, walking the streets drunk, she had been an easy target for a ruthless predator.

The Autumn of Terror Begins

Horrible as it was, this was not the first such murder to have occurred in the Whitechapel District, a slum in London's East End. Less than a month earlier, on August 7, a woman named Martha Tabram had been found dead of 39 stab wounds. And that previous April, a woman named Emma Smith had been violently attacked by three men and died in the hospital of her wounds. Like Nichols, both Smith and Tabram had been prostitutes. One theory was that a so-called High Rip gang was working in the neighborhood, blackmailing prostitutes for money and murdering those who did not pay up. But now with this latest crime, the public began to fear that a maniac was on the loose in Whitechapel and that it would be only a matter of time before his next attack.

At first, the killer was known simply as "The Whitechapel Murderer" or "The East-End Fiend." Then, on September 27, 1888, the Central News Agency of London received a letter. It claimed to be from the killer and was signed "Jack the Ripper." The grisly nickname quickly caught on in the press and has stuck to this day.

The fall of 1888 would become known as the Autumn of Terror as

BREAKING NEWS: On August 31, 1888, the Star ran this headline after the discovery of Nichols's body: "A REVOLTING MURDER. ANOTHER WOMAN FOUND HORRIBLY MUTILATED IN WHITECHAPEL. GHASTLY CRIMES BY A MANIAC."[3]

the unknown killer continued to prowl the East End, leaving at least four more bodies in his wake. Despite a lengthy investigation and numerous leads, the police were never able to solve the crime. It remains one of the most famous unsolved mysteries of all time: the chilling case of Jack the Ripper.

Chapter 2

London's Mean Streets

In 1888, Great Britain was a wealthy empire with colonies all over the globe. London, the capital, was a bustling metropolis of some 4 million people. But amidst all the glittering prosperity was also utter poverty, much of it concentrated in London's East End. It was here, in the dark streets of the Whitechapel District, that the Ripper committed his bloody deeds.

The East End had pockets of good and bad neighborhoods, but in its worst areas it was a dirty slum plagued by crime. The area's population had swelled with recent immigrants, including many Irish seeking a better life and Jews fleeing ethnic persecution in eastern Europe.

This influx of
people led to terrible
overcrowding, and
it was common for
six or eight people to
live in a single room.
In addition to
the overcrowding was
a lack of sanitation, which bred disease. Up to
55 percent of children in the East End died before
the age of five. Those who survived often suffered
abuse, neglect, and poverty. Children fell off their

"I assure you I found nothing
worse, nothing more degrading,
nothing so hopeless, nothing
nearly so intolerably dull and
miserable as life in the East End
of London."[1]

—Victorian author
Thomas Henry Huxley

Many of the poor children who lived in the East End
of London were not able to afford shoes.

seats in school, so weak from hunger they could not learn.

In a time of economic depression and high unemployment, families could do little to improve their situation. Men often worked as builders, as butchers in slaughterhouses, or as dock laborers carrying coal or grain. Sometimes they were so hungry from the heavy labor, they could not finish a full day's work. Women found jobs in sweatshops sewing clothes or making matchboxes, working as many as 17 hours a day for no more than ten pennies or a shilling. Others made extra money selling handmade goods in the market. But when they could not make ends meet, some women had no choice but to turn to prostitution. Police estimated there were approximately 1,200 prostitutes in Whitechapel in 1888.

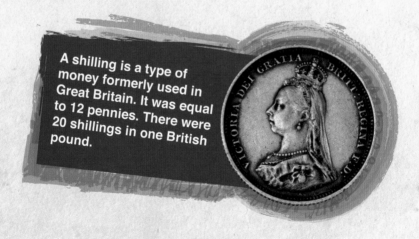

A shilling is a type of money formerly used in Great Britain. It was equal to 12 pennies. There were 20 shillings in one British pound.

Prostitution and Victorian Society

British society during the reign of Queen Victoria (reigned 1837–1901) was very conservative. It was a time when it was considered improper for a lady to show even her ankles in public. People did not feel comfortable talking about prostitution. Part of the reason why the Ripper's killings were so shocking was because his victims were all prostitutes. The crimes forced people to think and talk about social problems that were usually not discussed in polite society.

Because of the conservative attitudes of the day, some people believed that the Ripper's victims got what they deserved. After all, they said, these were immoral

Booth's Survey of Life in the East End

Charles Booth, a philanthropist who conducted a survey of poverty in the East End of London in 1889, identified various classes of people living in the area. These included the poor, the very poor, and the lowest level, which he described as "occasional laborers, criminals, and semi-criminals."[2]

The poor held jobs at very low wages, from 18 to 21 shillings per week. This was barely enough to support their families, and they struggled to make ends meet. The very poor had less than full-time employment, perhaps three days a week, and were in an even worse state than the poor. The lowest level was made up of people who were unemployed or only occasionally employed. These lived "the life of savages," according to Booth, "with vicissitudes of extreme hardship, and their only luxury is drink."[3]

19

Poor Treatment

In 1902, American writer Jack London stayed in an East End workhouse while conducting an undercover investigation about how the poor were treated in London. He wrote a book about the terrible conditions, entitled *The People of the Abyss.* In it, London reported that people staying in the workhouse ate the food left over from sick people in hospitals and slept in rooms infested with rats and other vermin.

women who drank gin and walked the streets at night. Perhaps the Ripper was doing society a favor by killing them off. However, few women willingly chose the life of prostitution. Instead, they were driven to it by the harsh conditions of their lives, made more difficult by broken marriages and alcoholism. With little or no education and few skills, they were unable to find or hold a decent-paying job and turned to selling their bodies as a last resort. It was often the only way to feed their children or to find a place to sleep for the night.

Workhouses and Lodging Houses

In the East End, thousands of people lacked a permanent home. They either slept on the street or found temporary shelter in workhouses and lodging houses. At a workhouse, people did manual labor, such as breaking up rocks or hauling trash, in exchange for some food and a place to sleep.

Those who could raise the money—approximately four pennies for a bed or eight pennies for a room—could stay at a lodging house. The conditions there were often miserable. In *The Bitter Cry of Outcast London,* Andrew Mearns describes some typical scenes:

> *Every room in these rotten and reeking tenements houses a family, often two. In one cellar a sanitary inspector reports finding a father, mother, three children, and four pigs! In another room a missionary found a man ill with smallpox and his wife recovering from her eighth [pregnancy], and the children running about half naked and covered with dirt. Here are seven people living in*

Many of London's poor slept in miserable conditions.

one underground kitchen, and a little dead child lying in the same room. . . . Where there are beds they are simply heaps of dirty rags, shavings or straw, but for the most part these miserable beings find rest only upon the filthy boards.[4]

When the Ripper murders began, reformers used the opportunity to expose the squalor and degradation of the East End in hopes of bringing about social change. Newspaper articles about the murders included vivid descriptions of the sad lives of the poor. Some claimed it was no wonder such ghastly conditions would produce the horror known as Jack the Ripper.

Romance and Reality

The popular image of Jack the Ripper in the media today is rather romanticized. Films, books, and television shows depict a well-dressed man in a top hat and dark cape, stalking a beautiful woman on a foggy gaslit street. The reality, however, was quite different. The Ripper's victims were mostly women in their forties, rough from hard living. The streets of Whitechapel were dirty and smelly. And there was nothing romantic about the brutality of the Ripper's crimes. Still, the romantic image persists as part of the legend and myth surrounding the infamous case.

Whoever he was, Jack the Ripper sparked great fear and anxiety in Victorian London because he represented a threat to the social order. He seemed to be the embodiment of lower-class wrath against the system—a grim warning to high society that the problems of the poor could not be ignored forever.

The Nemesis of Neglect

Reformers attributed crime, represented by a ghostly figure, to poverty and other social ills. The editorial cartoon was printed in *Punch* magazine with this poem:

> The Nemesis of Neglect.
>
> "There floats a phantom
> on the slum's foul air,
>
> Shaping, to eyes
> which have the gift of seeing,
>
> Into the spectre
> of that loathly lair.
>
> Face it—for vain is fleeing!
>
> Red-handed, ruthless,
> furtive, unerect,
>
> The murderous crime—
> the nemesis of neglect!"[5]

Chapter 3

The Killer Strikes Again

After the murder of Polly Nichols, police quickly formed an investigative team. The case fell under the jurisdiction of Sir Charles Warren, commissioner of the Metropolitan Police at Scotland Yard. Warren, along with Assistant Commissioner for Crime Robert Anderson, assigned two top detectives to head up the investigation, Chief Inspector Donald Swanson and Detective Inspector Frederick Abberline. However, police had no suspects, no motive, and nothing to go on. And before they could even catch their breath, the killer struck again.

On Saturday, September 8, only eight days after Nichols's death, an elderly wagon driver named John Davis prepared to leave for work. It was just before 6:00 a.m. when he stepped out into the backyard and saw something that shocked him to his core.

Sir Charles Warren

Demented Doctor?

When police surgeon Dr. George Bagster Phillips conducted a post-mortem examination at the Whitechapel Mortuary, he discovered that something else was missing from Chapman's body besides her brass rings. Bizarrely, the killer had removed her uterus. Noting the clean cuts that were used to remove this organ, Dr. Phillips suspected the murderer was a surgeon. "Obviously," he told the medical journal *Lancet*, "the work was that of an expert—of one, at least, who had . . . knowledge of [medical] examinations."[1] Although other doctors later disagreed with him, Phillips's comments caught on in the press, and the idea that the Ripper was a demented doctor has persisted to this day. Because body parts were removed from several other victims as well, some Ripperologists have even theorized that the murders were done specifically for the purpose of collecting organs for research.

There, in the backyard of the house at 29 Hanbury Street—only half a mile (0.8 km) away from where Nichols had been found—lay the body of a dead woman, Annie Chapman. The scene was even more grisly than that of Nichols's murder. Chapman's throat was cut with a gash so deep it had almost severed her head. Her abdomen, too, had been slashed open. Again, there was no sign of a struggle. Her face was swollen and her tongue protruded slightly, evidence she might have been strangled before being cut.

At her feet, the killer had laid what was likely the contents of the dead woman's pockets: a piece of coarse cloth, a small-tooth comb, and a pocket comb in a paper case. Near her head was a torn envelope containing two pills. Marks on her fingers showed that the brass rings she habitually wore had been wrenched off. They were never found.

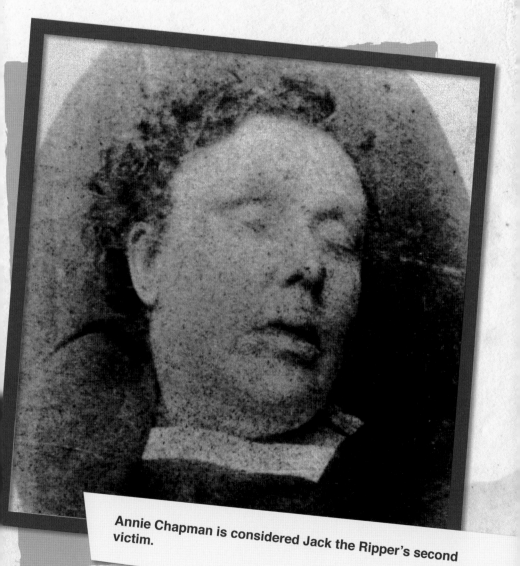

Annie Chapman is considered Jack the Ripper's second victim.

"Dark Annie"

Annie Chapman was 47 years old and homeless, staying at lodging houses with the money she could manage to earn on the street. Like Nichols, Chapman—or "Dark Annie," as her friends called her—was a prostitute. Five feet (1.5 m) tall and stout, she had a bulbous nose and a few teeth missing. A hard life and years of alcohol abuse had left her in very poor health. The doctor who examined Chapman's body said she had suffered from diseases of the brain and lungs that would have killed her in a few years.

Chapman's life had not always been so bleak. She had been married once and had three children. However, one child died and another was sent to live in an institution because of a disability. Both she and her husband, John Chapman, drank heavily, and eventually they separated, although he continued to send her a small allowance. He died in 1886, and Annie was left to struggle alone. Her friend Amelia Palmer observed that after her husband's death, "she seemed to have given way all together."[2]

On the night before her death, Chapman was not feeling well. Aside from her chronic illnesses, she had recently been in a fight with another woman at her lodging house over a bar of soap, and she was still a bit sore and bruised. However, with no money for a bed, she had no choice but to walk the streets, and she left the lodging house just before 2:00 a.m.

Chapman's Final Hours

At 4:45 a.m., a man named John Richardson came out onto the back steps at 29 Hanbury Street, overlooking the yard where Chapman's body would be found a little more than an hour later. The yard was empty, and Richardson saw nothing unusual. His testimony indicates that Chapman was almost certainly still alive at that time.

Some 45 minutes later, around 5:30 a.m., Elizabeth Long saw a woman who looked like Chapman standing near the house at Hanbury Street. She heard the man say, "Will you?" and the woman's reply, "Yes."[3] The man's back was to her, so she could not see his face, but she saw that he was dark-complexioned and looked foreign. He was wearing a brown deerstalker hat and a dark coat.

Several witnesses described the killer as wearing a deerstalker hat.

Long added that he looked to be more than 40 years of age, a little taller than Chapman, with a "shabby genteel" appearance.[4] If the witness can be trusted, then it is almost certain the man she saw was the killer. Moments after Long saw them, they probably slipped into the yard together.

Around the same time, Albert Cadoche, a young carpenter living at 27 Hanbury Street, heard voices coming from the yard next door. "No!" he heard a woman say.[5] A few minutes later there was a thud, as if something had fallen against the fence. If it was Chapman's body, then the time of death could be fixed at around 5:30 a.m., approximately a half hour before the murder was discovered. At that time it was already daylight, and there were people all around. The killer could have been disturbed at any moment. And after his gory work, he might have been covered in blood, which would have been noticed by anyone who saw him on the street. But yet again, he vanished without being seen.

Leather Apron

The police combed the yard for clues. One object they found seemed to have special significance. It was a leather apron, such as one that might be worn by a tradesman or a butcher, lying recently washed and soaked with water not far from where the body was found. This clue immediately directed their attention to a suspect.

The suspect was John "Jack" Pizer, a Jewish shoemaker in his late thirties nicknamed Leather Apron because of the work apron he always wore. Pizer was said to have been robbing and beating prostitutes in the area, and, according to a source quoted in the *Star* newspaper, he was a sinister-looking man who carried a knife and was "unquestionably mad."[6] When it was reported that a leather apron had been found near Chapman's body, the public was convinced he was the killer.

Hearing of the public outcry against him, a frightened Pizer went into hiding among his relatives. It was not until September 10

"Cool Impudence and Reckless Daring"

At the inquest, coroner Wynne Baxter offered the following description of how he imagined Chapman had been killed:

"After the two had passed through the passage and opened the swing door at the end, they descended the three steps into the yard. . . . The wretch must have then seized the deceased . . . by the chin. He pressed her throat, and while thus preventing the slightest cry, he at the same time produced insensibility and suffocation. There was no evidence of any struggle. . . . The deceased was then lowered to the ground. . . . Her throat was then cut in two places with savage determination, and the injuries to the abdomen commenced. All was done with cool impudence and reckless daring."[7]

Prejudice and the Search for the Ripper

The story of Leather Apron is a good illustration of how ethnic prejudice hampered the search for the Ripper. Although there was no real evidence against Pizer, many Londoners were only too ready to believe in his guilt simply because he was a foreigner—a Polish Jew. During the 1880s, Jewish refugees from eastern Europe had flooded the East End. Because these new arrivals spoke their own language and dressed differently, they were regarded with suspicion and resentment by the local population—and, when the Ripper murders began, they were singled out as scapegoats. According to a newspaper report, onlookers at the scene of Chapman's murder were heard to say that "no Englishman could have perpetrated such a horrible crime . . . it must have been done by a Jew."[9] This attitude was typical of many locals at the time and may have made it easier for the real killer—if he was a fair-skinned Englishman—to escape unnoticed while everyone was watching for a dark, foreign-looking suspect.

that police found and arrested him on suspicion of murder. The newspapers proclaimed, "They've captured Leather Apron!"[8]

However, their triumph was short-lived. Pizer was able to provide a solid alibi for his whereabouts on the nights of both Nichols's and Chapman's murders. Police also learned that the leather apron found in the yard belonged to the son of one of the tenants and had no link to Pizer. After a day and a half, Leather Apron was released. Police were back to square one.

Desperate to find the culprit, police rounded up a number of local men who were mentally ill or had committed violent crimes. Acting on the opinion of Dr. George Bagster Phillips that the killer had medical knowledge, Inspector Abberline began questioning medical students who had a history of mental illness or erratic behavior. All the inquiries led to a dead end, however. Weeks passed and police were no closer to finding the killer.

Newspapers reported the arrest of Leather Apron, proclaiming him the perpetrator of the Whitechapel murders.

Chapter 4

Double Event

Three weeks passed with no new information in the case. And then, on September 27, 1888, a taunting letter in red ink arrived at the Central News Agency of London. It claimed to be from the killer, and it was signed "Jack the Ripper." The letter promised, "You will soon hear of me with my funny little games. . . . My knife's so nice and sharp I want to get to work right away if I get a chance."[1]

Police doubted the letter was genuine. They had already received hundreds of messages like it and believed they were all hoaxes sent by pranksters or by members of the press attempting to spark a hot story. But three days later, the eerie

The *Illustrated Police News* provided a graphic depiction of the two murders.

promises of the letter came true when the killer acted again—this time committing two murders in one night.

The Berner Street Victim

The first body was found just after 1:00 a.m. on the morning of Sunday, September 30, lying in a courtyard off Berner Street. On one side of the yard was a workmen's club where people were singing and dancing. Outside, it was pitch dark. Louis Diemschutz, who worked at the club, turned his pony and cart in through the gates. Suddenly, the pony shied to the left as if avoiding something in its path. Diemschutz got down from his wagon and saw the huddled figure of a woman.

Diemschutz rushed into the club for assistance. He came out with a second man, and, shining a candle over the body, they confirmed it: she was dead, with blood flowing from an ugly gash in her throat.

Police Constable Henry Lamb arrived moments later, and Dr. Frederick Blackwell was called to the scene. The woman's body was still warm, leading the doctor to guess she had not been dead more than 20 minutes. "She looked as if she had been laid quietly down," Lamb noted.[2]

Unlike the others, this victim had not been cut in the abdomen—suggesting the killer had been interrupted in his work when Diemschutz arrived. Somehow, he had been able to disappear from the yard amid all the commotion. Where he went

Two Teams Collide

On the night of his double murder, Jack the Ripper crossed a boundary from the East End into the City of London itself. So while the previous murders were all under the jurisdiction of Warren and the Metropolitan Police, the murder of Catherine Eddowes was in City Police territory. City of London Police Commissioner Major Henry Smith immediately formed his own team of detectives to work the Ripper case. Now, with two separate teams on the hunt, the investigation got much more complicated. Officials from the two camps argued over methods and did not always share information as they should.

next was not a mystery, however. Three-quarters of a mile (1.2 km) away and less than an hour later, the Ripper left behind another body.

Mitre Square

At approximately 1:44 a.m., Constable Edward Watkins of the London City Police entered Mitre Square, a quiet and deserted cobblestone square surrounded by warehouses. He had last passed through the square only 15 minutes earlier and had seen nothing, but now as he shone the beam of his lantern about the area, he glimpsed a terrible sight:

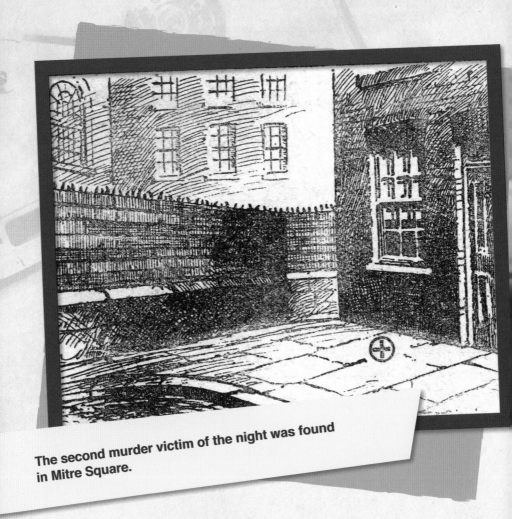

The second murder victim of the night was found in Mitre Square.

I saw the body of a woman lying there on her back with her feet facing the square [and] her clothes up above her waist. I saw her throat was cut and her bowels protruding. The stomach was ripped up. She was laying in a pool of blood.[3]

Not only were the stomach and throat cut, but—for the first time—the killer had also attacked his victim's face. It was as if the killer, frustrated at being disturbed the first time, had taken out all his rage on his second victim.

The alarmed constable ran for help, summoning a night watchman and alerting other police officers with shrill bursts of his whistle. A doctor guessed from the warmth of the body that the woman had not been dead more than 15 minutes. When the body was examined in the mortuary, it was discovered that the killer had again removed the uterus and, this time, had also taken the left kidney. Again, the skill and speed with which these organs were removed suggested the killer might be familiar with anatomy and strengthened suspicion against doctors, medical students, and butchers.

Doctors believed the killer used a knife similar to this one, now on display in a Jack the Ripper museum exhibit in London.

"Long Liz" and Kate Eddowes

By the following day, police had identified the victims. The Berner Street victim was a 45-year-old Swedish woman named Elizabeth "Long Liz" Stride. Despite her nickname, she was a small woman, only approximately five feet two inches (1.6 m) in height, with blue-gray eyes, dark brown hair, and a few front teeth missing. Police records in Gothenburg, Sweden,

Elizabeth Stride

listed her as a prostitute in 1865. The following year, Stride immigrated to England to work as a domestic servant. She married in 1869 and had children, but separated from her husband some time later and, at the time of her death, was living with a man named Michael Kidney.

A Killer's Timeline

On the morning of September 30, the Ripper killed two women in the space of an hour. Here is a timeline of events:

11:45 p.m.–12:30 a.m.—Elizabeth Stride is seen by three different witnesses on Berner Street talking to a man.

12:45 a.m.—Stride is seen being pushed to the ground by a man. She screams.

1:00 a.m.—Stride's body is found in a yard off Berner Street.

1:35 a.m.—Kate Eddowes is seen talking to a man near Mitre Square.

1:45 a.m.—Eddowes's body is found.

Occasionally, when the couple quarreled, she would leave Kidney to stay in a lodging house at Flower and Dean Street, earning money through prostitution. On September 29, Stride was seen leaving the lodging house at approximately 6:00 or 7:00 p.m. in the evening. She told nobody where she was going, but possibly she was going out to drink, as she often did. She may have been returning to the lodging house later that night, but along the way she met with the Ripper.

City police identified the second victim as 46-year-old Catherine "Kate" Eddowes. She was approximately five feet (1.5 m) tall, thin, and had auburn hair and hazel eyes. Those who knew Eddowes described her as a jolly woman who was often heard singing. Eddowes earned money through various methods, working for families, selling items on the street, and laboring on farms. She was overly fond of drink, and when money was tight, she also worked as a prostitute.

Kate Eddowes

Eddowes had three children with a man named Thomas Conway, who was possibly her husband. Eventually, he abandoned her because of her excessive drinking, and she took up with another man, John Kelly. On the night before Eddowes's death, she told Kelly she was going out to beg some money from her daughter. At 8:30 p.m. that evening, however, she was lying drunk on the street and was taken to a cell at the police station to sleep it off. By 1:00 a.m., she had sobered up and the police let her go—at the very hour when Jack the Ripper was on the hunt for his next victim.

Clues and Witnesses

Police quickly searched the area around the two murder sites, and, for the first time, they found a clue. At the foot of a stairwell along Goulston Street was a piece of an apron, wet with blood as if it had been used to wipe off the murder weapon. The piece was torn from the apron of Eddowes—meaning that it was certainly dropped by the killer himself.

THE BLOODY APRON: The spot where the piece of bloody apron was found suggests the killer fled back into the heart of the East End—another clue that the Ripper was probably not an outsider to the neighborhood but a man who lived in the area.

In addition to these clues, there were for the first time multiple eyewitnesses. At least four people believed they had seen Stride in the hour prior to her death. Two of them, William Marshall and James Brown, each thought they had seen Stride with a man on Berner Street at approximately 11:45 p.m. Marshall said the man was kissing Stride and said to her, "You would say anything but your prayers."[4] Brown overheard Stride say, "Not tonight, some other night."[5] Both witnesses put the man's height at approximately five feet and six or seven inches (1.6 or 1.7 m) and described him as wearing a dark coat. Marshall said the man was wearing a round cap with a small peak, "something like what a sailor would wear."[6] Brown noted that his coat was long and reached almost to his heels.

The next witness was a policeman. Constable William Smith was on Berner Street between 12:30 and 12:35 a.m. when he saw the victim talking to a man approximately five feet seven or eight inches (1.7 m) tall, around 28 years old with a dark complexion and a small dark mustache. He wore a dark felt deerstalker hat and a black diagonal cutaway coat.

Possibly the most crucial witness was Israel Schwartz. He claimed to have seen Stride at approximately 12:45 a.m. struggling with a man in the gateway to the yard where she was found dead. The man threw her to the ground, and she screamed. Schwartz noticed the man was approximately 30 years old, five feet five inches (1.6 m) tall, with a fair complexion and small brown mustache, wearing a short dark jacket and black cap with a peak. If Schwartz's description is to be believed, he may have been the only person ever to see Jack the Ripper in the midst of a murder.

Did the Ripper Have an Accomplice?

The testimony of Israel Schwartz has led to speculation that more than one person may have been responsible for the Ripper murders. Schwartz claimed he saw a man push Stride to the ground shortly before her murder. The man then looked up and shouted something that sounded like "Lipski," a Jewish name. He could have been shouting at Schwartz, who was Jewish—or addressing an accomplice. Schwartz did not wait to find out but hurried away in fright. As he did so, he thought another man was running behind him. Could the second man have been in league with the Ripper? Working on this hunch, police searched the neighborhood for a man named Lipski but turned up nothing.

Yet another witness, Joseph Lawende, may have seen the killer just before his second murder of the night. Near Mitre Square at approximately 1:35 a.m., he saw Eddowes. She was with a man wearing a loose pepper-and-salt jacket and a gray cloth cap with a peak. He had "the appearance of a sailor."[7] Other witnesses reported seeing a suspicious-looking man with a short jacket and sailor's hat wiping his hands on a doorstep not far away.

The witness descriptions did not all match exactly—they described, for instance, different hats and different styles of coats—but there were enough similarities for police to believe they had all possibly seen the same man. They circulated the various descriptions in hopes that someone would come forward with more information.

As they scrambled for clues, police received another mocking note. It was written in the same handwriting as the September 27 letter, and again signed with the frightening nickname:

> *I was not codding dear old Boss when I gave you the tip, you'll hear about Saucy Jacky's work tomorrow double event this time number one squealed a bit couldn't finish straight off. ha not the time to get ears for police. thanks for keeping last letter back till I got to work again.*
>
> *Jack the Ripper*[8]

The letter arrived at the Central News Agency on October 1, the morning after the murders— when word of the "double event" had barely hit the newsstands. Could it have been from the killer?

In hopes that someone might recognize the handwriting, police posted copies of the letter and postcard at every police station and also sent them to the press. Now the killer had a name, and the public went mad with Ripper Fever.

Shifting the Blame?

Above the spot where the apron scrap was found was another potential clue, a message written in chalk. It read:

The Juwes are not
The men that
Will be
Blamed for nothing.[9]

Had the badly spelled message been written by the killer as he fled, in an attempt to throw blame for the murders on the Jewish immigrants who lived in the area? Metropolitan Police Commissioner Warren thought so, although today experts do not believe the killer did leave the message. Fearing it might lead to an outbreak of violence against local Jews, Warren ordered the message rubbed off immediately, before it could even be photographed. When the incident report was written, the police officer disagreed about the wording, and today several variations of the message exist. Later, his action would be harshly criticized as destruction of evidence, described by Major Smith of the City Police as "an unpardonable blunder."[10] However, the anti-Jewish feeling was so strong in Whitechapel that Warren may, in fact, have avoided riots by erasing the message quickly.

Chapter 5

The Fifth and Final Murder?

In the aftermath of the "double event," police were under more pressure than ever before to find the phantom killer. Investigators were doing all they could, but this was a case unlike any they had ever seen before. Scotland Yard had ample experience in solving murder cases in the crime-ridden East End, but these were more often than not cases of domestic assault, drunken brawls, gang violence, and robberies gone wrong. A serial killer who chose his victims at random, with no motive other than to kill, mutilate, and spread terror among the public—this was something completely different and baffling.

Police now launched an all-out manhunt. Officers went door-to-door conducting searches and making inquiries. Undercover detectives, some disguised as women, patrolled the streets

The Scotland Yard building served as the headquarters of the Metropolitan Police in London.

in large numbers. Desperate for a breakthrough, Commissioner Warren looked into the idea of using bloodhounds to track the killer's scent. The papers mocked his efforts, publishing silly cartoons that showed Warren being chased by dogs. The press and public accused the police of being hopelessly incompetent. Government officials were discussing the problem in Parliament. Even Queen Victoria had started asking questions. Warren resigned in defeat on November 8.

By then, a month had gone by with no new murders, and residents of Whitechapel began wondering if the Ripper had moved on. The next day, Friday, November 9, the Ripper committed what many believe to be his final, and most hideous, murder of all.

A Message from the Queen

"This new most ghastly murder shows the absolute necessity for some very decided action. All these courts must be lit, & our detectives improved. They are not what they [should] be."[1]
—Her Majesty Queen Victoria, in a November 10 letter to the Prime Minister expressing her frustration at the lack of progress in the Ripper case

50

Mary Kelly

At approximately age 24, Mary Kelly was younger than the Ripper's other victims, and she is said to have been pretty. Born in Ireland and raised in Wales, she had come to London to find work and ended up a prostitute. Similar to the others, Kelly liked to drink and often spent the money she earned on alcohol. At the time of her death she was several months behind on the rent for her small room at 13 Miller's Court. She had a live-in boyfriend, Joseph Barnett, but they had recently quarreled and he had moved out.

> "It is quite clear that nothing can be expected from the police, and that we may have 20 murders, as well as seven or eight, without their doing a single thing or making a single effort which will be fruitful for the public good."[2]
> —from an editorial in the *Star*, November 10, 1888

Kelly was with her friend Lizzie Allbrook between 7:30 p.m. and 8:00 p.m. on Thursday, November 8. At approximately 11:00 p.m. that night, she was seen in the Britannica pub talking to a young man. At 11:45 p.m., another prostitute named Mary Cox saw Kelly entering her room at Miller's Court with a different man. Kelly was then very drunk, and Cox heard her singing in her room between midnight and 1:00 a.m.

At 2:00 a.m., Kelly was back on the street again, where she asked a friend named George Hutchinson if she could borrow six pennies. Hutchinson had no money to lend her, and moments later he saw that Kelly had found another customer, one who looked rather wealthy. This was a man approximately 34 or 35 years old, with dark hair and eyes, a mustache curled at the ends and a "respectable appearance."[3] Hutchinson thought he looked foreign, possibly Jewish, and noticed that he carried a small parcel in his hand. The two laughed together, and Hutchinson heard the man say, "You will be all right for what I have told you."[4]

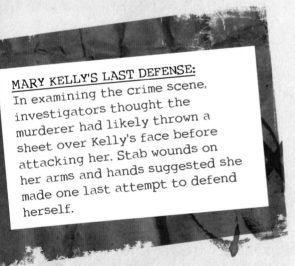

MARY KELLY'S LAST DEFENSE: In examining the crime scene, investigators thought the murderer had likely thrown a sheet over Kelly's face before attacking her. Stab wounds on her arms and hands suggested she made one last attempt to defend herself.

Curious about the well-dressed stranger, Hutchinson followed the pair back to Miller's Court. As Mary opened the door for her guest, she said, "All right, my dear, come along, you will be comfortable."[5]

Hutchinson waited around for approximately 45 minutes and then left.

At approximately 3:45 a.m., several women living in Miller's Court said they heard someone cry out "Murder!"[6] As this was not an unusual thing to hear in such a bad neighborhood, they ignored the cry—possibly the last word Kelly ever uttered in her life.

The Work of the Devil

Around 10:45 a.m., the landlord sent his assistant, Thomas Bowyer, to Kelly's room to collect her late rent, which was now up to 29 shillings. Bowyer rapped at the door and got no answer, so he peered through a broken window—where he saw a scene of pure horror. Bowyer fled to fetch the landlord, John McCarthy. "The sight we saw," McCarthy later said, "I cannot drive away from my mind. It looked more like the work of a devil than that of a man."[7]

Police arrived and found the door to the apartment locked; the key had apparently been

DEFENDING THEMSELVES: Police warned prostitutes to stay off the streets, but most continued to ply their trade, joking grimly that they might be next for the Ripper. Some began carrying weapons to defend themselves in case of an attack.

Bloodhounds

Bloodhounds are dogs specially bred for their ability to pick up a scent. First developed for hunting, the breed was found to be useful in the tracking of humans and is used around the world today by law enforcement. Their large nasal cavities enable the dogs to pick up a human scent from breath, sweat vapor, and skin cells or other particles, even days after a person has passed through an area. Their long, hanging ears and the folds of wrinkled skin around their faces help trap these scent particles. Once they pick up a scent, bloodhounds will follow it persistently, ignoring all other odors. They have been known to follow the trail of a person as far as 130 miles (209 km).

The usefulness of bloodhounds to solve crimes was well known in the 1880s. Scotland Yard had actually field-tested two hounds, Barnaby and Burgho, in the hopes that they could help catch the Ripper. However, they failed to make arrangements to purchase the dogs. When Inspector Abberline telegrammed a request that they be sent to Kelly's murder scene, they had been sent back to their owner and were not available.

lost some time before. Inspector Abberline ordered the area sealed off until bloodhounds could be sent. Unfortunately, the dogs were unavailable, and at last the door was broken down with a pickax.

On the bed lay Kelly's corpse. With the luxury of a private room where he had no fear of being seen and interrupted, the killer had taken the time to mutilate the body much more completely than ever before. Except for her eyes and hair, Kelly was completely unrecognizable. A photographer was called to document this horrific scene, as had not been done with any of the other murders.

A camera similar to this would have been used to photograph the scene of Kelly's murder.

Chapter 6

Ripper Fever

The Ripper had now killed five victims. Scotland Yard and the City Police kept extra forces on the street, casting a wide net over London. Meanwhile, the frenzy of panic and terror created by Jack the Ripper was at its height. Although the killings had all taken place within one mile (1.6 km) of each other, fear gripped the whole city and even the nation. Newspapers contributed to Ripper Fever by printing sensational stories about the murders, each one more bloodcurdling than the last. The story spread internationally, with Ripper headlines splashed across newspapers as far away as Italy and Argentina.

Police were overwhelmed with letters from the public offering advice about how to catch the killer and naming possible suspects. Soon investigators were tied up with numerous false leads—many, predictably, pointing the blame at foreigners or outsiders. At one point, police even interrogated several cowboys and Native Americans from the United States visiting London as part of a traveling show.

Five Victims Only?

One of the many questions surrounding the case of Jack the Ripper concerns the number of his victims. The murders of Mary Ann Nichols, Annie Chapman, Elizabeth Stride, Kate Eddowes, and Mary Kelly are generally considered to be linked because of the way the victims were killed.

But could there have been others? The following are sometimes named as Ripper victims: Emma Smith (killed on April 4, 1888), Martha Tabram (August 7, 1888), Alice McKenzie (July 17, 1889), and Frances Coles (February 13, 1891). Smith, however, was attacked by a group of men, and evidence strongly suggests the Ripper acted alone. Tabram was stabbed rather than having her throat cut, but even so, many believe she could have been Jack's first victim. MacKenzie's throat was cut and her abdomen mutilated, but not as severely as the Ripper's victims, while Coles's throat was cut, but her body was not mutilated. Police suspected these final two murders to be the work of a copycat killer, but only the killer himself knew for sure.

Letters from Hell

Among the endless flood of information the police had to sift through were letters supposedly sent by the killer himself. These came from all over the

Letter from the Ripper

The first use of the name "Jack the Ripper" appeared in the following letter, received by the Central News Agency on September 27, 1888:

Dear Boss,

I keep on hearing the police have caught me but they wont fix me just yet. I have laughed when they look so clever and talk about being on the <u>right</u> track. That joke about Leather Apron gave me real fits. I am down on whores and I shant quit ripping them till I do get buckled. Grand work the last job was. I gave the lady no time to squeal. How can they catch me now. I love my work and want to start again. You will soon hear of me with my funny little games. I saved some of the proper <u>red</u> stuff in a ginger beer bottle over the last job to write with but it went thick like glue and I cant use it. Red ink is fit enough I hope <u>ha. ha.</u> The next job I do I shall clip the ladys ears off and send to the police officers just for jolly wouldn't you. Keep this letter back till I do a bit more work, then give it out straight. My knife's so nice and sharp I want to get to work right away if I get a chance. Good Luck.

Yours truly
Jack the Ripper

Dont mind me giving the trade name

PS Wasnt good enough to post this before I got all the red ink off my hands curse it No luck yet. They say I'm a doctor now. <u>ha ha</u>[1]

world, written in different styles of handwriting. Most were obvious fakes. Three of them, however, captured police attention and are often named by experts today as possibly being from the killer. Whether genuine or not, these letters helped fuel Ripper Fever.

The first two letters of interest are the "Dear Boss" letter and "Saucy Jacky" postcard. These were sent on September 27 and October 1, just before and after the double murder of Stride and Eddowes. Both are in the same handwriting and are especially significant because they are the first to use the name "Jack the Ripper." Eerily, the "Dear Boss" letter refers to the killer's intent to "clip the ladys ears" in his next murder and send them to police—and part of Eddowes's ear was indeed clipped off.[2] However, no attempt was made to send her ears to the police, and it could have been coincidence.

Another reason to think the "Dear Boss" and "Saucy Jacky" notes could be real is the timing.

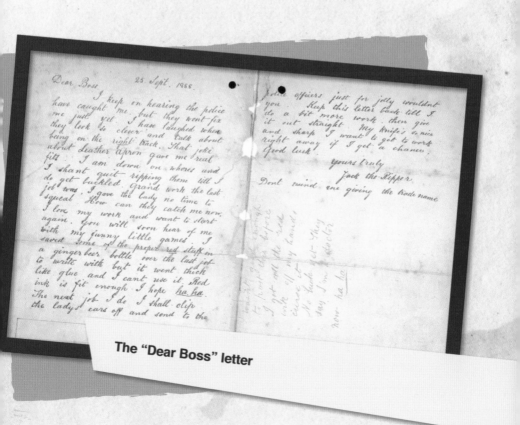

The "Dear Boss" letter

The "Saucy Jacky" postcard was received on October 1, when news of the double murder was not yet generally known. And yet it refers to the "double event." This, however, can be explained if the writer was, for instance, a member of the press who knew of the story before it broke. Certainly, the person who wrote those two letters had a way with words. The handwriting is that of an educated person, and the wording is clever—perhaps too clever, some experts say, to have been the work of an unhinged serial killer.

But on October 16, another piece of correspondence from the killer arrived. The letter was addressed "From Hell," and it was sent to Mr. George Lusk of the Whitechapel Vigilance Committee. This letter was more crudely written and contained spelling mistakes, as if written by a person of little education. It came along with a package containing a gruesome surprise: half a human kidney. "I send you half the Kidne I took from one woman," the letter boasted. "Tother piece I fried and ate it was very nise."[3]

The left kidney had been taken from the body of Eddowes on September 30, the night of the "double event." Could this have been Eddowes's kidney? If so, the letter was genuinely from the killer. Dr. Openshaw of the London Hospital Museum examined the organ, which had been preserved in alcohol. He confirmed that it was indeed human and that it had been removed from a body within the past three weeks. The kidney showed signs of Bright's disease, an alcoholism-related condition that

The Lusk Letter

From hell.

Mr Lusk,

Sor

I send you half the Kidne I took from one woman and prasarved it for you tother piece I fried and ate it was very nise. I may send you the bloody knif that took it out if you only wate a whil longer

signed
Catch me when you can Mishter Lusk [4]

Eddowes had suffered from. Still, there was no way of knowing for certain whether the kidney had belonged to Eddowes.

Inexplicably, after Kelly's murder, the killings stopped. The Autumn of Terror had ended. When the rest of November went by without event and winter passed with no new killings, the police wondered what had happened to the Ripper. He had left behind a lot of questions.

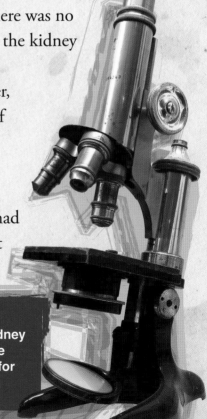

Dr. Openshaw likely used a microscope similar to this one to examine the half kidney supposedly sent by the killer. Without the ability to analyze DNA, he could not say for certain the kidney belonged to Eddowes.

Chapter 7

Profile of a Killer

There have been many theories, some convincing and some outlandish, concerning the identity of this infamous murderer. Although nobody knows for certain who Jack the Ripper was, an analysis of the crimes can provide some important clues. Over the years, various experts have come up with profiles, or descriptions, of Jack the Ripper based on his method of killing, the type of victims he chose, and other evidence.

Dr. Bond's Profile, 1888

One of the first profiles of the killer was offered by Dr. Thomas Bond, who performed the autopsy on the woman many believe to have been the Ripper's

One contemporary artist imagined what the capture of Jack the Ripper would look like. The artist chose to depict the Ripper with a beard, wearing sailor's clothes.

RELIGIOUS SYMBOLISM?: The locations of the murders on the map of Whitechapel are roughly in the shape of a cross. According to one theory, this is evidence that the killer was a religious person who felt he was doing God's work by killing immoral ladies of the night. Another theory holds the opposite: the killer was a practitioner of black magic and planned the murders in the shape of a cross as part of a Satanic ritual.

final victim, Mary Kelly, in November 1888. Based on the observations of doctors who felt the killer had some type of medical knowledge, police had been investigating butchers and medical students. However, Dr. Bond disagreed.

Bond sketched a portrait of what he thought Jack the Ripper was probably like and what motivated him to commit his crimes. He wrote:

> The murderer must have been a man of physical strength and of great coolness and daring. There is no evidence that he had an accomplice. He must in my opinion be a man subject to periodical attacks of Homicidal and erotic mania. . . . It is of course possible that the Homicidal impulse may have developed from a revengeful or brooding condition of the mind, or that Religious Mania may have been the original disease, but I do not think either hypothesis is likely.[1]

Bond also described the murderer's likely physical appearance:

The murderer in external appearance is quite likely to be a quiet inoffensive looking man probably middleaged and neatly and respectably dressed. I think he must be in the habit of wearing a cloak or overcoat or he could hardly have escaped notice

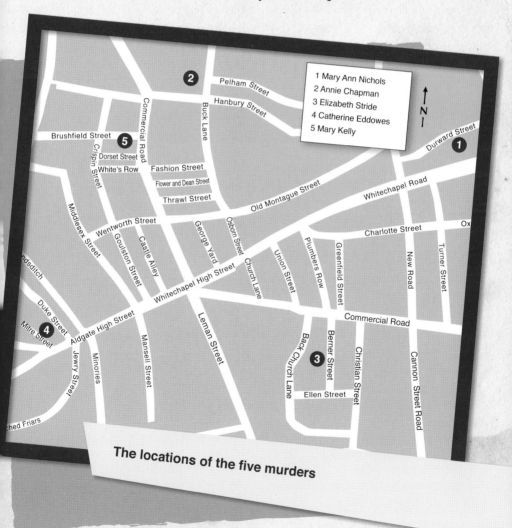

1 Mary Ann Nichols
2 Annie Chapman
3 Elizabeth Stride
4 Catherine Eddowes
5 Mary Kelly

The locations of the five murders

in the streets if the blood on his hands or clothes were visible. Assuming the murderer to be such a person as I have just described he would probably be solitary and eccentric in his habits, also he is most likely to be a man without regular occupation, but with some small income or pension.[2]

The FBI Profile, 1988

The use of criminal psychological profiles, developed by experts in criminal behavior, has become standard in law enforcement in recent decades. In 1988, 100 years after the murders, special agents John Douglas and Roy Hazelwood prepared their own criminal personality profile for Jack the Ripper. The agents had helped pioneer the use of modern psychological profiling for the FBI. In many

More Ape Than Man

In the late nineteenth century, Charles Darwin's theory of evolution had an influence on criminology, the study of criminal behavior. Certain types of criminals were believed to be in an earlier stage of evolution than ordinary human beings—that is, more ape than man. According to the theory of criminal anthropology, physical characteristics such as a strong jaw line, bushy eyebrows, and long arms were said to be signs that a person was more likely to commit crime. Because of such theories, and because of the ugliness of the murders, many people were convinced the Ripper would have an apelike or monstrous appearance. However, experts today agree it is more likely that he was a rather ordinary-looking person who would not have attracted attention or suspicion.

respects, the FBI agents agreed with Dr. Bond's conclusions. Following are some of their observations based on the crimes:

- Although there was no evidence of sexual assault, the crimes were sexual in nature and could be characterized as "lust murders."
- All the crimes took place on a Friday, Saturday, or Sunday, in the early morning hours, suggesting the killer had a regular job during the week.
- The killer did not necessarily have medical knowledge or surgical expertise but may have worked as a butcher, mortician's helper, medical examiner's assistant, or hospital attendant.

The FBI investigators found that the killer was most likely a white male 28 to 36 years of age and of a lower social class. They believed he would have been fairly neat and orderly in appearance— again, someone who would not have attracted attention. In intelligence he would have been average, not a criminal mastermind.

PROFILING: Modern psychological profiling was developed in the 1970s at the Behavioral Science Unit of the FBI Academy in Quantico, Virginia.

Jack the Ripper was probably single, never married, and never had a meaningful relationship with a woman. He was most likely a loner, someone who had difficulty relating to others, and he likely lived alone so that he would not be accountable to anyone for his comings and goings.

Based on his crimes and on the study of criminal behavior in hundreds of thousands of similar cases, the FBI agents also made some guesses about the killer's background and psychology. They felt he was likely the product of a broken home and was raised by a dominant female figure who drank heavily and had a variety of different male partners. She may have abused and neglected him, which would explain the killer's apparent hatred and fear of

Jill the Ripper

Although letters supposedly sent by the killer were signed "Jack," some suspected he could have been a she. One of those who supported this theory was Sir Arthur Conan Doyle, creator of the fictional detective Sherlock Holmes. Doyle suggested that the killer may have been a female midwife or abortionist—or a man disguised as one. As a woman, she would have been able to win the trust of her victims, thus making it easier for her to commit the killings. Furthermore, he noted, a midwife could be seen with bloodstains on her clothing without arousing suspicion. Inspector Frederick Abberline also considered this idea a possibility. John Douglas of the FBI rejected the idea that the killer might be a woman, noting that female killers like Jack the Ripper are extremely rare.

women. He killed and mutilated women in an attempt to get power and control that he never had as a child.

Whoever the Ripper was, why did he stop his killings? FBI profiler John Douglas notes that serial killers, as a rule, do not suddenly stop killing simply because they are tired of it or no longer feel the urge. There must have been some reason. Either the killer died, was thrown into jail or an asylum, or moved to another place far away—where he may have continued his crimes.

MO and Signature

Signature and MO, or modus operandi, are two important concepts used when discussing criminal behavior. According to FBI Special Agent John Douglas, "MO refers to the techniques the offender employs to commit the crime. Signature refers to the elements not necessary to carry out the crime, but what the offender has to do to fulfill his emotional needs."[3] In the case of Jack the Ripper, his MO was to quickly overpower and attack his victims by surprise. His signature was to mutilate the victims after death. The similar MO and signature in all five murders are what gave police the clue that all of the murders were committed by the same hand.

Chapter 8

The Suspects

"We are inundated with suggestions and names of suspects!"[1] wrote Commissioner Warren in 1888. The same is true today. New suspects for the crimes are still being proposed by Ripperologists. Could any of these suspects, new or old, have been the Ripper?

Montague John Druitt

In a memo written in 1894, Metropolitan Police Chief Constable Melville Macnaghten listed M. J. Druitt among the top three people suspected by police at the time of the murders. According to Macnaghten, Druitt's own family thought he was the Ripper. Today, he is still one of the main suspects named by Ripperologists.

Druitt was a young, good-looking lawyer and teacher who came from a good family. However, he was a very troubled man. His mother was in a

M. J. Druitt

mental institution, and Druitt feared that he, too, might be going insane. On or around November 30, 1888, he was dismissed from his teaching position for an unknown reason. One theory is that he was homosexual and had inappropriate relationships with some of his students, but no evidence exists to support this. Whatever the cause of the firing, it threw him into despair. A few days later, he committed suicide by drowning himself in the Thames River.

After Druitt's suicide, the Ripper murders stopped. But was he the killer? His father was a doctor, so he could have had access to medical knowledge and tools, and he had an office in the East End, near the scene of the murders. At age 31, with dark hair and a respectable appearance, he fit some eyewitness descriptions of the Ripper. In addition, he was mentally unstable. On the other hand, Druitt had no known history of violent behavior. Also, psychological profiling of serial killers suggests that such killers rarely take their own lives. The case against Druitt, then, is far from certain.

IN SEARCH OF . . .: Based on witness descriptions, police were looking for a man between five feet five inches and five feet eight inches (1.6 and 1.7 m) in height, between the ages of 28 and 40, and possibly foreign in appearance.

Aaron Kosminski and Nathan Kaminsky/David Cohen

The second possible suspect named by Macnaghten was a Polish Jew named Kosminski. Macnaghten describes him as follows:

> *This man became insane. . . . He had a great hatred of women, specially of the prostitute class, & had strong homicidal tendencies: he was removed to a lunatic asylum about March 1889. There were many circumstances connected with this man which made him a strong "suspect."*[2]

In his memoirs, Sir Robert Anderson, assistant commissioner and head of Crime Investigation at the time of the murders, claimed police knew the real identity of the Ripper but they were unable to prosecute the suspect. Notes made by Chief Inspector Donald Swanson indicate that Kosminski was identified as the Ripper by an eyewitness, but the witness refused to testify against him because he was a fellow Jew. If this is true, then the case against Kosminski is very convincing.

Ripperologist Martin Fido researched Kosminski in the late 1980s and found more information about the suspect. His full name was Aaron Kosminski, and he was a Jewish hairdresser, age 26, living in Whitechapel. Kosminski spent time in the

Colney Hatch Asylum. Paranoid and delusional, he had refused to accept food from anyone and instead ate bread he found in the gutters. He had once threatened his sister with a knife and, in the institution, attacked an attendant with a chair. However, other than these two incidents, there was no evidence that he was particularly violent or had the "homicidal tendencies" mentioned by Macnaghten.

Fido uncovered another Polish Jew named Nathan Kaminsky who was approximately the same age as Kosminski and had also been admitted to a mental institution, under the name David Cohen. Unlike Kosminski, he was extremely violent and had to be kept in restraints. Fido believed police had gotten the two mixed up and that the more violent and antisocial Kaminsky/Cohen may have been the Ripper.

Michael Ostrog

The third suspect mentioned by Macnaghten was Michael Ostrog. Macnaghten describes him as "a Russian doctor, and a convict, who was subsequently detained in a lunatic asylum as a homicidal maniac."[3] In fact, Ostrog was a thief and a con man. He was never convicted of killing anyone, only defrauding people of money. He was probably not really a doctor,

although he might
have pretended
to be one. He
was also probably
not really insane
but pretending
to be in order
to avoid a long
prison sentence.
In addition, at
five feet eleven
inches (1.8 m)
and more than 50
years old, he does
not match witness

Lost Records

When the Ripper case was closed
in 1892, Scotland Yard's files were
officially closed for a period of 100
years. When they were reopened to
the public in 1992, many of the files
were missing, fueling suspicions of
cover-ups and conspiracies. Some
researchers have claimed that the
police knew the murderer's identity all
along and intended to keep it a secret
by destroying the documents. In fact,
many of the papers were destroyed
due to bombing during World War II
(1939–1945), lost to souvenir hunters,
or tossed during the cleaning up of files
to make room for new documents.

descriptions. Although police at the time did question
Ostrog and considered him a serious suspect, most
Ripper experts today believe he would not have been
the right type of person to commit the murders.

George Chapman
(Severin Klosowski)

Inspector Frederick Abberline, who knew more
than almost anyone about the Ripper case, pointed
the finger at a different suspect—Polish immigrant
George Chapman, hanged in 1903 for poisoning.

Between 1897 and 1902, Chapman had a succession of mistresses, including Mary Spink, Bessie Taylor, and Maud Marsh. One after the other, the women died of mysterious stomach ailments. When Marsh died, a postmortem showed a poison, metallic antimony, in her system. The other two women were exhumed from their graves. Their bodies were hardly decomposed, proof that they, too, had been poisoned with antimony, a powerful preservative.

The more police learned about Chapman, the more they suspected him to be the Ripper. He was abusive of women, and he had attempted to kill his first wife with a knife in 1891 or 1892. A sharply dressed man, he fit the description given by George Hutchinson of the man seen with Mary Kelly on the night of her death, and as a foreigner, he matched other descriptions as well. He had studied medicine and surgery. Inspector Abberline was convinced Chapman and the Ripper were one and the same.

But poisoning is a very different type of crime than killing and mutilating with a knife. Could the type of person who committed the Ripper murders have changed his MO so completely? The FBI profile suggests it is unlikely, though investigators cannot rule it out.

Ripper suspect George Chapman poisoned at least three women.

Francis Tumblety

Another suspect with ties to the United States was Francis Tumblety, a quack doctor and con man who made money selling phony medicines. Tumblety openly despised women, and, bizarrely, he kept a collection of human uteruses preserved in jars. Tumblety was in London during the time of the

The Ripper in New York

On the night of April 23–24, 1891, aging prostitute Carrie Brown was murdered and mutilated at a hotel in New York City. The *New York Times* proclaimed that this was "a murder like one of Jack the Ripper's deeds."[4] If Brown can be counted among the Ripper's victims, then possible suspects might be George Chapman, who lived in New York and New Jersey from 1891 to 1892, or Francis Tumblety, who was known to have traveled between London and New York.

murders and was arrested by police on November 7, 1888, for several instances of indecency with other men. It was reported that Scotland Yard also suspected Tumblety of being the Ripper, but he jumped bail and escaped back to the United States before he could be charged with any crime.

Was Tumblety the Ripper? At the time of Kelly's murder, he was in police custody, but he could conceivably have killed the others. However, at approximately age 55 and five feet ten inches (1.8 m), he was older and taller than any of the men described by witnesses. He was also very probably homosexual. FBI profilers note that serial killers typically target the people they are attracted to, so Tumblety is therefore not as likely to be the killer as some of the other suspects on the list.

Dr. Roslyn D'Onston

Robert Donston Stephenson—alias Dr. Roslyn D'Onston—was a very odd man and an intriguing suspect. Two authors, Melvin Harris and Ivor Edwards, have named him as the man most likely to have been the Ripper. At the time of the murders, D'Onston was a patient at London Hospital, only a few blocks away from where Nichols's body was found. A doctor trained in Paris, France, he associated with prostitutes and was said to practice black magic. D'Onston became somewhat obsessed with the case, writing letters to the police and to the newspapers explaining his theories on how and why the murders were committed. Was he merely an interested observer, or could he himself

Organized and Disorganized Killers

In studying many different serial murderers, John Douglas and Roy Hazelwood of the FBI came up with two main types of offenders: the organized and disorganized types. The organized type of killer appears to function well in society, but deep down he has no feeling for anyone but himself. He is cunning and plans his crimes in advance, often hiding the bodies to avoid being caught. The disorganized type is a loner who cannot interact well with others. He does not plan his crimes but acts on impulse, like a wild animal on the hunt. He often takes foolish risks because he cannot control his urges. Douglas and Hazelwood found that Jack the Ripper fit the disorganized personality type. This means he would be someone more like Kosminski, not like the slick con man Tumblety or the scheming poisoner, Chapman.

A Bloodthirsty Sailor

At the time of the murders, some people—including Queen Victoria herself—thought the killer might have been a sailor. Witnesses described a man with the appearance of a sailor, and furthermore, the dates of the killings seemed to match up with the arrival of cattle boats on the Thames River.

If the Ripper was a sailor, he could have slipped off his boat on the weekend, killed, and then made his getaway on the river while police scrambled to find him in town. If so, this would also explain other unsolved Ripper-style murders at seaports around the world. Modern authors including Trevor Marriott have explored this theory, although no one has put forth any specific names of suspects.

have been the Ripper? At age 47, D'Onston was too old to match any of the witness descriptions. Police at the time were aware of him and apparently did not find him very suspicious. Still, D'Onston's name continues to come up on every list of Ripper suspects.

Prince Albert Victor, Duke of Clarence

Intriguing but unlikely theories about Jack the Ripper involve people at the very highest level of British society: the royal family. According to one of these theories, Prince Albert Victor, nicknamed "Eddy," the grandson of Queen Victoria and second in line to the throne, was secretly Jack the Ripper. Supposedly, the prince contracted syphilis, a sexually transmitted disease, while traveling abroad as a young man.

As the disease progressed, it made him go mad. The royal physician, Dr. William Gull, discovered him wandering about the streets of Whitechapel with blood on his hands. Realizing the prince was the Ripper, the royal family had him committed to an insane asylum, where he died of his disease in January 1892. Naturally, there was a cover-up and the public was allowed to continue believing the Ripper had never been caught.

Prince Albert Victor was not likely Jack the Ripper, but that did not stop the conspiracy theories.

There are some fragments of truth in this scenario. Prince Eddy could have fit witness descriptions, and he did die at the young age of twenty-eight—although the official cause of death was influenza, not syphilis. However, records show the prince was away from London during at least three of the murders. Police at the time never suspected him, and it was not until the 1960s that he became the subject of speculation. So while the tale of the royal Ripper makes a good story, it must be considered only a story.

The Royal Conspiracy

In another theory, the prince himself was not the Ripper but was unwillingly caught up in a royal conspiracy. While spending time in Whitechapel, the prince met and fell in love with Annie Crook, a local girl. They secretly married and had a child. Once Queen Victoria found out about the marriage, she took measures to break the pair apart.

Again there was a cover-up, and the royal physician had to eliminate everyone who knew about the marriage so the secret would never get out. Who knew the secret? The child's nurse, Mary Kelly, who told three other women, Polly Nichols, Annie Chapman, and Liz Stride. One by one, Dr. Gull killed them with the assistance of his coachman. Kate Eddowes, who also went by the name Mary Kelly, is said to have been killed by mistake.

Again, there is no evidence to back up this theory. There was indeed a person named Annie Crook and she did have an illegitimate daughter, but there is no proof that she knew Prince Eddy or was married to him. There is also no indication that any of the women killed by the Ripper knew either each other or Annie Crook. At the time of the killings, Dr. Gull was in his seventies and had suffered a stroke, which makes it difficult to imagine him out on the street committing brutal murders in the middle of the night, even with the help of another man. And finally, the grandson of Annie Crook later admitted that the whole story was completely made up. However, none of this has stopped people from being fascinated by the idea that the royal family was somehow involved in the Jack the Ripper crimes.

Jack the Ripper's Diary

In 1993, a book called *The Diary of Jack the Ripper* was published. It was supposedly the recently rediscovered diary of James Maybrick, a Liverpool cotton merchant who was secretly Jack the Ripper. According to the diary, Maybrick murdered prostitutes because he was angry about his wife being unfaithful. Also discovered with the diary was a ladies' gold watch engraved with the words "I am Jack J. Maybrick" and the initials of the five victims. The new finding excited Ripperologists until an analysis of the diary showed that it was likely an elaborate hoax, written in modern times in an old Victorian book.

Chapter 9

A Modern Look at the Crimes

In 1888, criminal investigation was not nearly as sophisticated as it is today. Although police did examine murder scenes for clues such as blood trails, footprints, or wheel tracks, they did not seal off the area or conduct as thorough an analysis as police would do today. Instead, they typically focused on removing the body as quickly as possible and cleaning up the blood. During the Ripper investigation, officers made mistakes and missed opportunities—for instance, when Commissioner Warren rubbed out a chalk message possibly from the killer before it could be photographed and when police failed to arrange for the use of bloodhounds. Fingerprinting was still a new idea, and police at the time failed to recognize its usefulness in solving crimes.

In addition, police and the public were hampered by an incomplete understanding of criminal behavioral psychology. They relied on racial prejudices as well as stereotypes of what a murderer would look like and how he or she would behave—

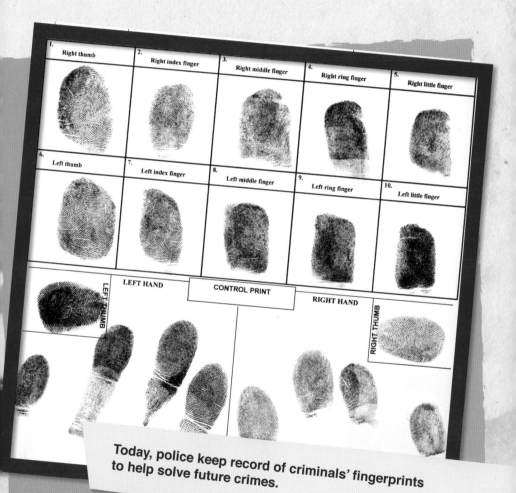

Today, police keep record of criminals' fingerprints to help solve future crimes.

for example, thinking that the Ripper would be monstrous in appearance or that he would definitely be a foreigner.

Looking back on the crimes from a modern-day perspective, can anything new be learned? Can increased scientific knowledge and up-to-date criminal tracking methods help solve the most famous cold case in the history of crime? And if not, how might these modern techniques have helped police solve the case if they had been available in 1888?

Fingerprinting

The technique of fingerprinting is key to placing a suspect at the scene of a crime. However, the technique was not used by law enforcement in Great Britain until approximately 1902. Had they been using fingerprinting in the 1880s, London police could have dusted for fingerprints in Kelly's apartment and compared any prints they found with those of suspects in the case. Police could have checked for fingerprints on the "Dear Boss" letter, the "Saucy Jacky"

FINGERPRINTS: No two people have the exact same fingerprints, not even identical twins.

postcard, and the letter and package "From Hell." The "Saucy Jacky" postcard, in fact, shows a fairly clear thumbprint, apparently in blood. If the letters were hoaxes, however, fingerprints could have led investigators in the wrong direction.

In recent years, author Patricia Cornwell has attempted to match fingerprints found in the Ripper letters with those of the artist Walter Sickert, who she believes was Jack the Ripper. Thus far, she has

Modern criminologists use a special dusting powder to find fingerprints. The dark colored powder sticks to the oils left behind by a person's hand.

The Bloody Thumbprint: A Lost Opportunity?

After copies of the "Saucy Jacky" postcard were shared with the public in October 1888, a man wrote to *The Times* suggesting that the bloody thumbprint be checked against the prints of suspects in the case. Police ignored the idea. Fingerprint evidence was not used to convict a criminal in Britain until 1902.

not been able to come up with a match because the samples found are not clear enough. But again, even if she were able to match Sickert's prints with those found on the letters, that would only prove that Sickert had authored the letters—not that he committed the crimes.

DNA Profiling

Deoxyribonucleic acid, or DNA, is an acid found inside human cells that carries a person's genetic material. Scientists can extract DNA from the cells of skin, hair, blood, saliva, and other bodily fluids and match it to a particular person with fairly high accuracy. This technique is called DNA profiling, or genetic fingerprinting. Today, when people are arrested or convicted of a crime, they may be required to provide a sample of their DNA, often from a swab of the mouth or a strand of hair. This DNA sample may be kept on file so police can use DNA evidence to connect them to future crime scenes.

DNA profiling did not become standard practice in law enforcement until the 1980s, nearly 100 years after the Ripper's crimes. Had it been available back then, it would almost certainly have been useful in the Jack the Ripper case. Police could have checked the crime scenes carefully and collected any physical evidence suspected to be from the killer. For instance, if one of the women had scratched the killer's arm, there might have been some of his skin cells embedded under her fingernails. Or, if the murderer had accidentally nicked himself with his knife, some of his blood might have been found at the scene. The DNA from these samples could then have been compared with the DNA from any murder suspects. It might not have helped catch the killer, but it could have quickly ruled people out.

DNA testing would have allowed police to determine for certain whether the half kidney sent to Lusk really belonged to Eddowes. If it were found to be a genetic match, then police would have known the package really came from the killer. They may have been able to check for DNA on the letter and package itself—for example, in saliva found on the stamp or skin cells inside the envelope.

In the television documentary *Revealed: Jack the Ripper, the First Serial Killer*, investigators looked for DNA on a shawl believed to have belonged to Eddowes. Unfortunately, so many years had gone by that all the DNA evidence had disappeared or decayed. Had the shawl or any other clothing worn by the victims been examined in 1888, usable samples might have been found that could have helped crack the case.

Composite Sketches

Sketches based on witness statements have long been used to help solve crimes. Two such suspect sketches appeared in the *Illustrated Police News* on October 20, 1888. However, their accuracy is questionable. They appear to be more like caricatures of what a brutal killer might look like rather than pictures taken from detailed witness descriptions.

Today, composite sketches are often made with the help of sophisticated computer programs that contain examples of every type of facial feature. For instance, if a witness says a suspect's eyes are deep set, the program could provide an example. Whether sketches are made by a skilled artist or with the help of a computer program, the close participation of eyewitnesses is essential. With the witness watching, minor adjustments are made to the sketch until it most closely matches the person he or she recalls seeing. Had police in 1888 been able to elicit an

Modern analysts created this composite sketch of Jack the Ripper.

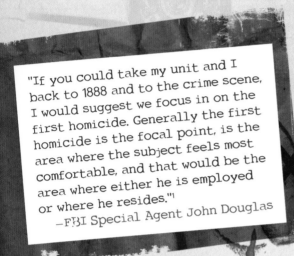

"If you could take my unit and I back to 1888 and to the crime scene, I would suggest we focus in on the first homicide. Generally the first homicide is the focal point, is the area where the subject feels most comfortable, and that would be the area where either he is employed or where he resides."
—FBI Special Agent John Douglas

accurate sketch of the man seen by witnesses such as Hutchinson, who got a very close look at the man with Kelly on the night of her death, it certainly could have helped them catch the killer.

Psychological Profiling and Geoprofiling

Modern psychological profiling has helped Ripperologists to make more educated guesses about which suspects in the Ripper case were more likely to have committed the crimes. Also known as offender profiling or criminal profiling, this technique relies heavily on behavioral psychology to paint a picture of what an offender might be like based on his or her crimes. Such profiling is only useful in determining the *type* of person who committed the crimes—it cannot identify a specific individual. However, combined with other techniques, it can be key to catching a killer. Once a suspect is caught, psychological profiling can also provide law enforcement with good techniques for questioning that will be most likely to result in a confession or sharing of information.

Geographic profiling, or geoprofiling, is a technique developed by Kim Rossmo of Texas State University to help determine the likely location of an offender's home based on the location of his or her crimes. "Most criminals operate out of their home in terms of their search for criminal targets," Rossmo explains. "Criminals commit crimes close to where they live—but not too close. They're affected by concerns over anonymity and not wanting to hunt in an area where they might be identified."[3]

If police in 1888 had had access to geoprofiling, it would have confirmed what they already suspected: the killer was not an outsider to the area but lived or worked in Whitechapel. It may have encouraged them to continue their door-to-door searches

"The police at the time were hampered ... by the fact that they had no experience of serial sexual murderers. They had no files to look at. They had no reliable consultants who could come along and say 'It'll be a man like this, look for this sort of man.' They were therefore looking for the traditional madman: someone who was sort of foaming at the mouth or had a vacant stare."[2]
—Crime historian Melvin Harris

Modern Geoprofiling

In 1998, a geographic profile for Jack the Ripper was produced by Rossmo and his team for a television documentary. The crimes were all committed within a mile of each other. When the locations of the sites were fed into Rossmo's computer program, the results indicated the killer likely lived in the vicinity of Flower and Dean Street and Thrawl Street.

in the very specific areas of Flower and Dean Street and Thrawl Street.

An Enduring Mystery

Today, more than 120 years since the Jack the Ripper killings, thousands flock to London to tour the East End, revisiting the scenes of the crimes and following the murderer's trail.

Although the true identity of Jack the Ripper may never be known, the search continues. If the past few decades are any indication, the list of suspects will continue growing as more research is done concerning the Ripper crimes. Lost documents relating to the case may be rediscovered. Some suspects who were considered by police at the time, such as Michael Ostrog, will likely be eliminated thanks to this additional research and modern psychological profiling. Perhaps in the future, groundbreaking techniques in criminology will be able to shed new light on the case.

Perhaps the case of history's most infamous serial killer will never be solved. But then again, the solution is not the point—it is the mystery itself that continues to fascinate.

Tools and Clues

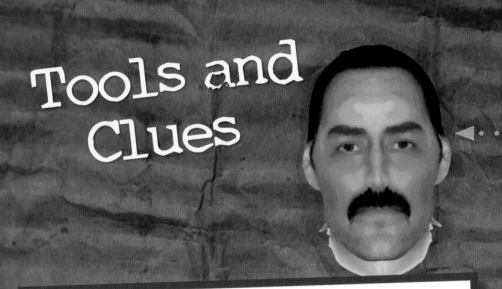

Nineteenth-Century Tools and Clues

<u>apron—</u> A piece of bloody apron, possibly used to wipe off the killer's knife, was left on Goulston Street after the murder of Eddowes.

<u>letters from Hell—</u> Numerous letters were received by police, one sent along with half of a human kidney—but were these notes really from the killer?

<u>message in chalk—</u> A mysterious message in chalk was left on a wall where the piece of Eddowes's apron was found: "The Juwes are not the men that will be blamed for nothing."

<u>photography—</u> Although it was not yet standard practice to photograph a crime scene, it was done in the case of Kelly's murder.

<u>publicity—</u> Bills were posted in public places and handed out in the neighborhood alerting people to be on the lookout and to come forward with any information.

undercover detectives—	Detectives dressed in plain clothes, and often in women's clothes, hoping to observe the killer.
witness accounts—	Several witnesses who may have seen the Ripper described a man five feet five inches to five feet eight inches (1.6 to 1.7 m) in height, between the ages of 28 and 40, and possibly foreign in appearance.

Twentieth-Century Tools and Clues

DNA evidence—	Experts looked for DNA on the shawl of victim Eddowes but were unable to extract a usable sample for analysis.
fingerprints—	Experts have examined fingerprints left on several letters supposedly sent by the killer but no definitive link has yet been found.
geographic profiling—	Researchers have examined the location of each crime to theorize where the suspect likely lived and worked.
police records—	Modern Ripperologists study police records that have been reopened to the public, scouring for new connections between the clues and the victims.
psychological profiling—	Researchers have examined the details of each crime to create a profile of what type of person likely committed the crime.

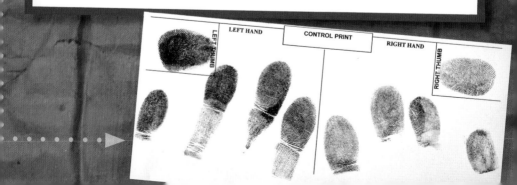

1888   Emma Smith is attacked by a gang of men on April 3 in the Whitechapel District; she dies in the hospital two days later.

1888   Martha Tabram is murdered in the Whitechapel District on August 7.

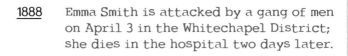

1888   Mary Ann "Polly" Nichols is found dead in Buck's Row on August 31.

1888   Annie Chapman is found dead at 29 Hanbury Street on September 8.

1888   John Pizer, a.k.a. "Leather Apron," is
        arrested and questioned on September 10
        but is released when his alibi is
        verified.

1888   The body of Elizabeth Stride
        is found in Berner Street on
        September 30.

1888   Catherine Eddowes is found dead
        in Mitre Square on September 30,
        45 minutes after Stride.

1888   On October 1, police make public
        a letter and postcard supposedly
        written by the killer, both signed
        "Jack the Ripper."

1888   George Lusk of the Whitechapel
        Vigilance Committee receives a package
        on October 16 labeled "From Hell,"
        containing a letter and half a human
        kidney.

1888   Police Commissioner Sir Charles Warren
        resigns under public pressure on
        November 8.

Timeline

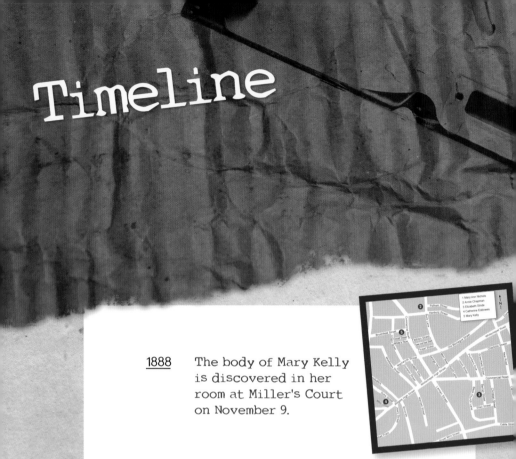

1888   The body of Mary Kelly is discovered in her room at Miller's Court on November 9.

1888   In November, Dr. Thomas Bond writes a description of what might have motivated the killer and who he could have been.

1888   M. J. Druitt is fired from his teaching job on November 30. He commits suicide a few days later and becomes a suspect.

1891   Carrie Brown is murdered in New York City in a similar manner to the Ripper's victims.

1892   The Ripper case is officially closed
and the case files sealed.

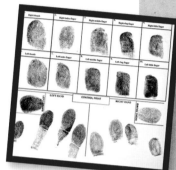

1902   Fingerprint evidence is
used to convict a criminal
in Great Britain for the
first time.

1903   Ripper suspect George Chapman is hanged
for poisoning three women.

1992   The Ripper case is reopened to investigators.

1993   *The Diary of Jack the Ripper* is published.
The book purports to be the diary of Jack
the Ripper but is revealed to be a hoax.

1998   Experts working for the FBI prepare
a criminal profile on Jack the Ripper.

Glossary

accomplice . . . . A partner in a crime.

alibi . . . . A claim made by a person accused of a crime to have been at another place when the crime occurred.

asylum . . . . An institution for the care of poor, sick, or mentally ill people.

autopsy . . . . The examination of a dead body to determine the cause of death.

constable . . . . A British term for a police officer.

coroner . . . . An official whose job is to investigate the cause of deaths.

inquest . . . . An official investigation to find the reason for something such as a person's death.

mortuary . . . . A place where dead bodies are kept prior to being cremated or buried.

mutilate . . . . To cut up or damage severely.

nemesis . . . . An enemy or rival.

postmortem . . . . An examination of a body after death.
examination

Ripperologist . . . . . A person who studies the case of Jack the Ripper.

scapegoat . . . . A person or group of people unfairly blamed for something that goes wrong.

Additional Resources

Selected Bibliography

Douglas, John, and Mark Olshaker. *The Cases That Haunt Us: From Jack the Ripper to JonBenet Ramsey, the FBI's Legendary Mindhunter Sheds Light on the Mysteries That Won't Go Away.* New York: Scribner, 2000. Print.

Evans, Stewart P., and Keith Skinner. *The Ultimate Jack the Ripper Companion: An Illustrated Encyclopedia.* New York: Carroll & Graf, 2000. Print.

Marriott, Trevor. *Jack the Ripper: The 21st Century Investigation.* London: John Blake, 2005. Print.

Rumbelow, Donald. *The Complete Jack the Ripper.* New York: Penguin, 2004. Print.

Sugden, Philip. *The Complete History of Jack the Ripper.* New York: Carroll & Graf, 1994. Print.

Further Readings

Begg, Paul, and Martin Fido. *The Complete Jack the Ripper A–Z.* London: John Blake, 2010. Print.

Gray, Drew D. *London's Shadows: The Dark Side of the Victorian City.* New York: Continuum, 2010. Print.

Werner, Alex, and Peter Ackroyd. *Jack the Ripper and the East End.* London: Chatto & Windus, 2008. Print.

Web Links

To learn more about Jack the Ripper, visit ABDO Publishing Company online at **www.abdopublishing.com**. Web sites about Jack the Ripper are featured on our Book Links page. These links are routinely monitored and updated to provide the most current information available.

Places to Visit

Jack the Ripper Walking Tours
Several companies offer guided walking tours of the East End of London where the Ripper murders occurred.

Museum of London
London Wall, London EC2Y 5HN
Tel: 020-7001-9844
Fax: 020-7001-1058
Email: info@museumoflondon.org.uk
http://www.museumoflondon.org.uk
The Museum of London displays exhibits about the history of London from prehistoric times until today. Visitors to the museum can learn more about life in the city during the Victorian Era, when Jack the Ripper was active.

Source Notes

Chapter 1. Murder in Whitechapel

1. "Brutal Murder in Whitechapel." *Daily News*. 1 Sept. 1888. *Casebook: Jack the Ripper*. Web. 3 July 2011.

2. Donald Rumbelow. *The Complete Jack the Ripper*. New York: Penguin, 2004. 28.

3. "A Revolting Murder." *Star*. 31 Aug. 1888. *Casebook: Jack the Ripper*. Web. 3 July 2011.

Chapter 2. London's Mean Streets

1. *Jack the Ripper: An On-Going Mystery*. Dir. Brian J. Kelly and Virginia Anita Williams. Discovery Channel, 2005. DVD.

2. "Poverty Maps of London." *Charles Booth Online Archive*. Library of the London School of Economics & Political Science. Web. 3 July 2011.

3. Ibid.

4. Donald Rumbelow. *The Complete Jack the Ripper*. New York: Penguin, 2004. 4–5.

5. "The Nemesis of Neglect." *Punch*. 29 Sept. 1888. *Casebook: Jack the Ripper*. Web. 28 Nov. 2011.

Chapter 3. The Killer Strikes Again

1. Philip Sugden. *The Complete History of Jack the Ripper*. New York: Carroll & Graf, 1994. 91.

2. "Annie Chapman." *Casebook: Jack the Ripper*. Casebook.org, n.d. Web. 3 July 2011.

3. Ibid.

4. Stewart P. Evans and Keith Skinner. *The Ultimate Jack the Ripper Companion: An Illustrated Encyclopedia*. New York: Carroll & Graf, 2000. 98.

5. Philip Sugden. *The Complete History of Jack the Ripper.* New York: Carroll & Graf, 1994. 96.

6. Philip Sugden. *The Complete History of Jack the Ripper.* New York: Carroll & Graf, 1994. 74.

7. Stewart P. Evans and Keith Skinner. *The Ultimate Jack the Ripper Companion: An Illustrated Encyclopedia.* New York: Carroll & Graf, 2000. 105.

8. Philip Sugden. *The Complete History of Jack the Ripper.* New York: Carroll & Graf, 1994. 143.

9. Donald Rumbelow. *The Complete Jack the Ripper.* New York: Penguin, 2004. 37.

Chapter 4. Double Event

1. "Ripper Letters." *Casebook: Jack the Ripper.* Casebook.org, n.d. Web. 3 July 2011.

2. Philip Sugden. *The Complete History of Jack the Ripper.* New York: Carroll & Graf, 1994. 170.

3. Stewart P. Evans and Keith Skinner. *The Ultimate Jack the Ripper Companion: An Illustrated Encyclopedia.* New York: Carroll & Graf, 2000. 201.

4. Ibid. 165.

5. Ibid. 166.

6. Ibid. 165.

7. Ibid. 124.

8. "Ripper Letters." *Casebook: Jack the Ripper.* Casebook.org, n.d. Web. 3 July 2011.

9. Donald Rumbelow. *The Complete Jack the Ripper.* New York: Penguin, 2004. 60.

10. Philip Sugden. *The Complete History of Jack the Ripper.* New York: Carroll & Graf, 1994. 254.

Chapter 5. The Fifth and Final Murder?

1. Stewart P. Evans and Keith Skinner. *The Ultimate Jack the Ripper Companion: An Illustrated Encyclopedia.* New York: Carroll & Graf, 2000. 357.

2. "What We Think." *Star.* 10 Nov. 1888. *Casebook: Jack the Ripper.* Web. 3 July 2011.

3. Stewart P. Evans and Keith Skinner. *The Ultimate Jack the Ripper Companion: An Illustrated Encyclopedia.* New York: Carroll & Graf, 2000. 376–377.

4. Philip Sugden. *The Complete History of Jack the Ripper.* New York: Carroll & Graf, 1994. 334.

5. Ibid. 334.

6. Ibid. 329.

7. Ibid. 316.

Chapter 6. Ripper Fever

1. "Ripper Letters." *Casebook: Jack the Ripper.* Casebook.org, n.d. Web. 3 July 2011.

2. Ibid.

3. Ibid.

4. Ibid.

Chapter 7. Profile of a Killer

1. Stewart P. Evans and Keith Skinner. *The Ultimate Jack the Ripper Companion: An Illustrated Encyclopedia.* New York: Carroll & Graf, 2000. 361.

2. Ibid. 362.

3. John Douglas and Mark Olshaker. *The Cases That Haunt Us: From Jack the Ripper to JonBenet Ramsey, the FBI's Legendary Mindhunter Sheds Light on the Mysteries That Won't Go Away.* New York: Scribner, 2000. 47.

Chapter 8. The Suspects

1. Philip Sugden. *The Complete History of Jack the Ripper.* New York: Carroll & Graf, 1994. 467.

2.Donald Rumbelow. *The Complete Jack the Ripper.* New York: Penguin, 2004. 142.

3. Ibid.

4. Philip Sugden. *The Complete History of Jack the Ripper.* New York: Carroll & Graf, 1994. 464.

Chapter 9. A Modern Look at the Crimes

1. *Jack the Ripper: The Phantom of Death.* A&E Television Networks, 1995. Television.

2. Ibid.

3. *Revealed: Jack the Ripper, The First Serial Killer.* Dir. Dan Oliver. Atlantic Productions, 21 Nov. 2006. Television.

Index

Abberline, Frederick, 24, 33, 54, 68, 75, 76
Anderson, Robert, 24, 73
Autumn of Terror, 14, 61

Baxter, Wynne, 31
Blackwell, Frederick, 36
Bond, Thomas, 62, 64–65, 67
Booth, Charles, 19
Bowyer, Thomas, 53
Brown, Carrie, 78

Chapman, Annie, 26–32, 57, 82
Chapman, George, 75–76, 78, 79
clues, 7, 26, 30–32, 43, 47, 84
Cohen, David, 73–74
Conway, Thomas, 43
Cox, Mary, 51–52

Davis, John, 25
Diemschutz, Louis, 36–37
D'Onston, Roslyn, 79–80
Doyle, Sir Arthur Conan, 68
Druitt, M. J., 70–72

East End of London, 6, 13, 14, 20, 22, 32, 37, 43, 48, 72, 94
living conditions, 16–18, 19
Eddowes, Catherine "Kate", 37, 40, 41, 42–43, 45, 57, 59–61, 82, 89–90

FBI profile, 66–69, 76, 78, 79, 92

Great Britain, 16, 86

Hutchinson, George, 52–53, 76, 92

Kaminsky, Nathan, 73–74
Kelly, John, 43
Kelly, Mary, 51–55, 57, 61, 64, 76, 78, 82, 86, 92
Kidney, Michael, 41
Kosminski, Aaron, 73–74, 79

Lamb, Henry, 36
Lambeth Workhouse, 9–11
letters, 14, 34, 36, 46–47, 57–61, 68, 79, 86–88, 89, 90
London, Jack, 20

Macnaghten, Melville, 70, 73–74
McCarthy, John, 53
Mearns, Andrew, 21
Metropolitan Police, 24, 37, 47, 70

Neil, John, 7
news coverage, 9, 14, 22, 31–32, 34, 46–47, 56, 58, 60, 90
Nichols, Mary Ann "Polly", 11, 13, 14, 24–28, 32, 57, 79, 82
nicknames, 14, 46

Ostrog, Michael, 74–75, 94

Palmer, Amelia, 28
Parliament, 50
Phillips, George Bagster, 26, 33
Pizer, John "Jack", 31–32
prostitution, 11, 18–20, 41

Queen Victoria, 19, 50, 80, 82

Ripper Fever, 47, 56, 58,
royal conspiracy, 82–83

Scotland Yard, 24, 48, 54, 56, 75, 78
Smith, Emma, 14, 57
Smith, Henry, 37, 47
Stride, Elizabeth "Long Liz", 40–41,
   44, 45, 57, 59, 82
suspects, 70–83

Tabram, Martha, 13–14, 57
tools
   bloodhounds, 50, 54, 84
   composite sketches, 90, 92
   DNA profiling, 88–90
   fingerprinting, 86–88
   geoprofiling, 92–94
   photography, 47, 55, 84
   psychological profiling, 66, 72,
      92–94
Tumblety, Francis, 77–79

Victor, Prince Albert, 80–81

Warren, Sir Charles, 24, 37, 47, 50,
   70, 84
Watkins, Edward, 37
Whitechapel District, 7, 13–14, 16,
   18, 22, 26, 47, 50, 60, 64, 73,
   81–82, 93
witness accounts, 11, 29, 30, 44–45

About the Author

Jennifer Joline Anderson has been writing since she was a teenager, when she won a contest and had her first short story published in *Seventeen* magazine. Today she lives with her husband and two children, Ruby and Henry, in Minneapolis, Minnesota, where she writes and edits educational books for young people. Her recent books for ABDO Publishing include *John Lennon: Legendary Musician and Beatle* and *Essential Events: The Civil Rights Movement.*

About the Content Consultant

Dr. Drew Gray is a senior lecturer at the University of Northampton in the United Kingdom. He teaches history and criminology and is the author of London's Shadows: The Dark Side of the Victorian City and other books and articles on the history of crime in London. He is a Londoner who knows the East End well.

Photo Credits

Popperfoto/Getty Images, cover, 3, 42, 99 (bottom); Universal History Archive/Photolibrary, 7, 25, 81; Express Newspapers/Getty Images, 10, 27, 40, 98 (top), 98 (bottom), 99 (top); Hulton Archive/Getty Images, 12, 63; Ray Roberts/Alamy, 17; Solodov Alexey/Shutterstock Images, 18; The British Library/Heritage Images, 21; The Print Collector/Photolibrary, 23; Dorling Kindersley/DK Images, 29; INTERFOTO/Alamy, 33, 71; English School/The Bridgeman Art Library/Getty Images, 35; Mary Evans Picture Library/Alamy, 38; Akira Suemori/AP Images, 39; AP Images, 49; PA Wire URN:5455662/Press Association/AP Images, 50; Mike Dabell/iStockphoto, 54; Shutterstock Images, 55, 96 (bottom), 105; The National Archives/Photolibrary, 59; Zsolt Horvath/Bigstock, 61; Red Line Editorial, 65, 100; Trinity Mirror/Mirrorpix/Alamy, 77; Hans Laubel/iStockphoto, 85, 97, 101; Peter Kim/iStockphoto, 87; HO Channel 5 Broadcasting/AP Images, 91, 96 (top)